NEVER ~~NEW~~ NORMAL

First edition July 2020

Book design by Authorsupport.com

ISBN 978-1-7353975-0-4 (paperback)

ISBN 978-1-7353975-1-1 (ebook)

Published by VCOpress

www.gregverdino.com

NORMAL

Uncommon Ideas
for Leaders
Who Won't Settle
for the Status Quo

GREG VERDINO

Co-creator of *The Adapt Manifesto*

"The greatest danger in times of turbulence is not the turbulence; it is to act with yesterday's logic."

—PETER DRUCKER

"The way you have always done business
is the way you will go out of business."

—GREG VERDINO

WELCOME

In October 2010, the journalist Joe Weisenthal tweeted that, in order to avoid excessive fluff and filler most books should be articles, most articles should be blog posts, and most blog posts should just be tweets. That was just a few months after McGraw-Hill published my first book, *microMARKETING: Get Big Results by Thinking and Acting Small*, and I'm proud to say that it could never have been an article. I crammed in so many ideas about modern marketing that even ten years later I have little left to say about that particular topic.*

Other topics, though? I have plenty to say.

---

* And seriously, other marketing thought leaders have written entire books and entrepreneurs have built entire businesses based on ideas I relegated to a mere mention in one sub-chapter or another. For example, ideas about why brands should love their haters and why micro-influencers would one day turn out to be where social media marketing magic happens (ahem).

Even so, it took me eight years to write this book. By Weisenthal's standard, and in my own defense, I'd argue that this isn't just one book after all, but 16 entire books' worth of material rolled into one.

You see, it's a collection of 16 blog posts and articles (I've spared you my tweets)—15 of which were previously published between 2012 and 2019,[*] and one of which appears here for the first time. A greatest hits collection, of sorts, that touches on strategy, innovation, change, transformation, technology, the future, and more. And for all of that, it's a deliberately short book. The kind of book you can read in a few hours and in any order you like. Within reason, that is...

There's no overarching narrative to pull you from chapter to chapter. There's not even a single, definitive point-of-view. Eight years have given me plenty of opportunities to learn, unlearn, relearn, and rethink. But there

---

[*] Presented here with a bit of editing (to correct obvious errors and remove most of the woefully outdated references) but otherwise intact and free of fluff.

is a loose theme that ties many (but not all) of the pieces together: *Wait-and-see is a two-step plan for achieving organizational obsolescence.*

Whoa, that's rough. But no matter how uncertain things seem right now, we can't lean on the crutch of inaction. The old normal isn't coming back, and there won't be some new normal to take its place. Instead, we must step boldly toward a future that will bear little resemblance to our present and for which our past is no longer a reliable predictor of what to expect.

Welcome to the *Never Normal*.

IDEAS INSIDE

NEVER NORMAL

"Only a crisis—actual or perceived—produces real change. When that crisis occurs, the actions that are taken depend on the ideas that are lying around."

MILTON FRIEDMAN

Nobody had a novel coronavirus on their digital transformation BINGO card. And yet, it was the onset of the COVID-19 pandemic and the resulting economic turmoil—rather than AI, blockchain, cloud, or the Internet of Things (or competitive pressure from Airbnb, Uber, Tesla, Lemonade or even Amazon)—that drove a host of both small *and sweeping* changes in how business gets done, practically overnight.*

---

* For clarity, in no way am I diminishing the massive human, social, emotional and economic toll of the COVID-19 pandemic. My focus in this piece though is on how businesses can forge ahead in times of great

While it might be a stretch to give COVID full credit for driving so many organizations toward digital, the virus' ability to accelerate the inevitable certainly proved more powerful than many an organization's ability to ignore the inevitable and many leaders' attempts to hold the inevitable at bay for just *one. more. earnings. season.*

After years of planning, handwringing, skepticism and drawn-out processes during which (frankly) so little actually happened, we all woke up one morning in 2020 to a world that had been radically transformed—suddenly, and in many ways, irreversibly. And while you could hardly say that everything turned out "OK", it would be disingenuous to argue that many of the things that changed were sacred or that the changes themselves weren't far easier done than said.

Overnight, home became the place we work. Gig workers became essential workers. Universities realized they could evaluate students on their merits without the

---

uncertainty. So yes, I know that I am focusing in on only one (arguably small, inarguably rosy) part of the bigger picture.

aid of standardized testing, then educate those students without them ever arriving on campus. Financial services companies—from mortgage lenders to auto insurers—were forced to be fair(er) and even a wee bit more flexible. Hollywood suddenly (*surprise!*) figured out how to retool their entire distribution model to allow film fans to experience opening night from the comfort of their couch, as music's biggest stars and your hometown's smallest concert venue woke up to the potential of streaming events. The world learned to Zoom.

Yes, I'm deliberately focusing on the positive (assuming you view progress as positive), and I'm well aware of the darker disruptions brought about by this crisis. But are these things not examples of the workforce, customer experience, business model, organization-wide, and industry-level innovations we were talking about when we were talking about digital transformation all along? And are these the "ideas that are lying around" that economist Milton Friedman suggests we cast about for and finally act upon when crisis spurs us to change?

If so, why didn't more organizations act sooner? Perhaps Friedman's view that a perceived crisis is enough to produce real change was too charitable. Perhaps only a *true* crisis would do. After all, by failing to adapt sufficiently to technology-driven change over time, traditional industries and legacy organizations turned after-the-fact digital transformation into a crisis of their own making—and even then, largely failed to act with the urgency it implied.

It's sad that it took a pandemic to prove once and for all that transformation talk is cheap and that the real action is in—well—*action*. And so, after years of pretending that they had *even more years* before disruption would be imminent, of fooling themselves into believing that tech-driven innovators were merely interesting edge cases, of resisting risk-taking, and persisting in the notion that digital transformation is uncertain even when its upside should have been clear, so many organizations flipped the switch on their future.

Now, I'm not saying that digital transformation is

as clear-cut as this one-and-done adjustment we've all just gone through. That it's as trivial as equipping our (white collar) employees to work from home, even if today's remote work policies plant the seeds for a more radical rethink about the nature of work and the value of human capital.

Transformation is, of course, more profound than that. But I do think it's time we admit that one big thing we got wrong about digital transformation is how easy it could be to get it more-or-less right—certainly in smaller doses, but even as a larger program as more organizations found themselves rapidly reworking their ecommerce strategy, business model, distribution channels, and supply chain. It would be fair to say that post-COVID, digital transformation as a mythology is dead while the transformative power of delivering meaningful change to better meet your constituents' evolving needs has survived its demise.

* * *

It never should have taken a crisis of global proportions to spur so many organizations into action. The alternative would have been far more palatable for most.

What if, instead of biding their time before a rushed and radical reinvention, these same organizations had spent the last decade (or two) gradually adapting to the environment that had quite clearly been changing around them the entire time? What if seeing change led more leaders to do more than merely *say* their organizations might one day change? What if more traditional organizations had seen a budding digital revolution as strategic white space, and not waited until they saw the whites of their enemies' eyes—only to ultimately realize that they were looking at their own self-imposed obsolescence in the rearview mirror?

In that scenario, I suspect we would be less breathless about total transformation. Had leaders been more serious about driving change all along, their truly adaptive organizations would have been evolving at or near the pace of the environments in which they operate. Traditional businesses would have become digital businesses (no, that bar isn't high enough—would have become *better* businesses) gradually and over time. Less through the scorched earth campaign by which we 'disrupt or die' and more through the steady spark of a strategy through which we 'adapt to thrive'.

* * *

Having seen that meaningful change can less risky, more realistic, more reasonable, and even repeatable, I'm hopeful that a greater portion of business decision makers will see the logic in making always-on adaptability a core competency for themselves, their teams, and their organizations at-large.

And that's the good news in all of this, because today's trials are hardly the last ones we will endure during our lifetimes. The next crisis may be economic, environmental, social, political, or technological, rather than biological—but it will come (actually, it's already here...). The best businesses will anticipate and prepare, get ahead of the changes it will precipitate, blunt its blows, and rise in its wake. They will, as the United Marines would say, improvise, adapt and overcome.

For years, I've been saying that the *old normal* no longer exists but the *new normal* has yet to fully present itself, leaving both people and organizations in something of a liminal state that is more "*and*" than "*or*". Today, I would be quicker to say that we shouldn't expect a new normal at all. In fact, the worst thing any of us can do is hope for some new normal—a new period of relative stability, relative certainty—to arrive.

The truth is that we are entering a *Never Normal* in which the frequency and pace of disruptions to everything we know will require us all to be more adaptable than we'd ever imagined. A *Never Normal* in which an ability to repeatedly and reliably adjust to any new condition the world throws our way is the current state-of-play for modern organizations and a critical competency for the people who lead them. A *Never Normal* in which the only thing we can expect with any degree of certainty is that we will need to come to terms with the unexpected and the uncertain.

A *Never Normal* in which this much is clear:

The transformation any organization should have been aiming to achieve all along was not to merely become more digital but to become truly adaptable in the face of unrelenting and never-ending cycles of change. Because if we're being honest, rewarding the champions of the status quo was never really normal anyway.

Appearing in print for the first time, with inspiration drawn from adaptmanifesto.org, recent blog posts, and content from my current speech.

STEP BOLDLY

The next round of organizations to fail in the wake of disruption will do so not because their leaders didn't see the future coming, but because they failed to see their own organization's place in it.

I'm talking about companies that manufacture products as demand shifts to services, that focus on ownership as their customers demand access, that maintain their pipelines but lose ground to platforms. This is not because they don't see these shifts happening around them, but because they can't imagine what their company would look like if they actually leaned into these shifts to reinvent from within.

Arguably, this has always been the case. Blockbuster, Kodak, Nokia, Sony, and Xerox had early access to the innovations that would ultimately challenge their legacy lines of business. These innovations would have given those companies a glimpse of a different future, but may have seemed like little more than digital distractions from their cash cows.

Perhaps they were looking at technologies before their time, but the real problem lay in their inability to imagine what they could do to ensure that their own organizations could thrive in a world where these innovations had rendered their core business obsolete.

The difference, though, is that when their own moment of reckoning happened years ago (in some cases, a decade or more ago), their vision of the digital future would have been fuzzier than yours is today. All of this was so new. Things are different now. Even if you can't predict exactly what your market, industry, economy, or the world will look like in ten years' time, you're undoubtedly well past the point of questioning the importance of digital transformation as a survival strategy for your own organization. You know that today's exponential technologies will serve as basic building blocks for tomorrow's thriving businesses.

So, you're "doing digital". You're innovating at the edges or digitalizing the core. You're tapping into technology to build a leaner, meaner, faster or better version of the company you are today.

However, I'd suggest you're focusing on the wrong things. For many businesses, these kinds of initiatives are necessary, but they're not enough. They amount to little more than shoring up the past at a time when every business should be staking a claim for the future.

Too often, digital evolution is rooted in the assumption that your same old business can be extended into a novel new future. It's the kind of unchecked assumption that causes established businesses to double-down on legacy models and structures, outmoded practices, and risk-averse cultures, even if those things come to appear futureproofed by a bit of digital polish.

Despite *looking* more digital, your business remains stalled in its present or mired in its past. Then tomorrow's reality sets in: The way you've always done business becomes the way you go out of business.

What if, instead of inching towards tomorrow with incremental digitization, you were to step boldly into the future and truly transform?

This deceptively simple change in perspective can have a profound effect on the way you think about digital transformation. Rather than merely identifying all the ways in which digital can optimize your business as it operates today, imagine what your company would look like if it were born with digital DNA. Viewed through this lens, the future of your business will bear little resemblance to today's steady state.

The decisions you make and actions you take will extend well beyond digitizing the things that got you where you are today. Instead of starting with a laundry list of technology projects, start with a reason why, draw upon innovative business models, breakthrough strategies and entirely new forms of value, and end with a winning formula for thriving in the future and playing a vital role in creating it.

September 26, 2018, Raconteur Digital Transformation 2018, The Times of London

THE FUTURE IS NOT NOW

The future is, by definition, in the future. Sounds obvious enough, so why did I think it would be worth pointing this out?

I can't count the number of times I've heard or read a proclamation that "the future is now." That we are "living in the future today." That the future "has arrived." Everyone from the media to marketers, from analysts to futurists, revels in declaring that we are indeed living in tomorrow, today.

I myself have been fond of occasionally quoting William Gibson saying, "The future is already here, it's just not evenly distributed," although I take his point to be more about the uneven diffusion of innovation rather than about the early arrival of the day after tomorrow.

Don't get me wrong—"the future is now" is a nice bit of semantic shorthand to underscore the sense of marvel we feel upon recognizing that the things we speculated about years ago are the things we see all around us today. The "Minority Report" technology Philip K Dick imagined in 1956 is finding its way into our modern world through the efforts of Apple, the NSA, and the Chinese government. Dozens of technology manufacturers promise Rosie-like robots to take on our housework.* Artificial intelligence threatens to take our jobs on the one hand, and usher in a workers' paradise by taking on the routine drudgery on the other. If the rate of technological change is remarkable, the results of technological change can appear truly wondrous.

---

* *The Jetsons*—the animated series that introduced the world to Rosie, an automated, anthropomorphic household helper—was produced in the 1960s and aired through the 1980s. Most of today's robots aren't so sophisticated but Google 'household robots [year]' and you'll get a taste for what's on offer.

But sorry, the future is still not now.

"The future is now" carries just an air of the self-congratulatory "we have arrived." But in truth we have not arrived. While it is certainly true that the old normal no longer exists, it is equally true that the new normal has yet to even present itself*—assuming, of course, that we should even expect a new normal to ultimately emerge.** In the meantime, we are merely taking the first steps in what is destined to be a long journey.

If it's true that the last 10 years have delivered more change than the preceding 100, then it's equally true that each coming year will deliver more change than we've seen in the last 10 combined. We are living in an exponential era—progress greatly and increasingly outpaces the linear march of time. This is not the time to let ourselves off the hook. If the future is now, then we might be tempted to believe that the actual, chronological future (the one

---

* Ah, there it is – just like I mentioned in chapter one.

** Asked and answered.

coming next year or next decade) is meant to look like our actual, chronological today.

Worse, we might be satisfied to simply recreate today, all over again, rather than envision and create new futures. Better futures. More prosperous futures. Futures in which we solve the problems that plague the present.

To put this in a business context, this might amount to holding your ground instead of forging a new path—maintaining the same products for the same markets, taking last year's numbers and forecasting an additional 10%. Instead of identifying your next high growth opportunity—by anticipating changing market conditions and emerging consumer needs to innovate your products, to reinvent your business models, to evolve the experiences you deliver, and to exponentially increase the value you create.

If you don't reimagine your business for yourself, you will be reimagined out of existence by others. You will be disrupted. And you won't reimagine your business if you imagine that you've arrived at "the future" already.

Today, mobile devices account for a substantial majority of Apple's revenue—devices that did not exist before 2007, prior to which Apple was not even in the mobile business. Had Steve Jobs and his team not envisioned a future in which desktops and laptops would give way to tablets and handhelds, Apple might have remained little more than an also-ran computer company (with pockets of passionate fans for sure, but market share so small as to be insignificant). Had Netflix not foreseen the movement of media into the cloud and reimagined itself as a streaming service, it might have found itself chained to the sinking ship of physical DVDs. But they did reimagine themselves; so much so that they rendered their own prior business model archaic if not outright obsolete.

These were not the last reinventions we'll see from either of these organizations. Nor should your last reinvention (*what? you've not yet gone through a reinvention of your own?*) be your *absolute* last.

So, no. The future is not now. The future is *next*. But

while the future might not be now, it is created by the decisions you make and the actions you take today.

What's next for you?

February 14, 2014

ZEG

Zeg.

It's a Georgian word that has no English equivalent. Zeg is "the day after tomorrow." So, while the meaning is simple enough and we certainly have a full phrase to express it when we need to, evidently the concept is not so important for those of us who speak English as a primary language* as to warrant its own simple, elegant, three-letter word.

Right? Wrong.

The concept is vital. And since this is a business book and I'm no linguist, my newfound discovery of an old Georgian word has inspired me not to lobby for yet

---

* I'd suspect the same is true for speakers of most other languages too.

another addition to the Oxford Dictionary but instead to assert that a clear-eyed vision for what *zeg* really means should be at the very core of your business.

Thinking about *zeg* forces business leaders to adopt a futures orientation—to think about what not only tomorrow but the day *after* tomorrow will look like; consider what challenges and opportunities will present themselves; and muster the courage to make the right decisions today given our foresight into the future that is arriving faster by the minute.

Thinking about *zeg* fuels innovation. It gives us the drive to imagine how the wants and needs of our consumers, constituents, collaborators, and communities may one day be different than they are today; and the confidence to anticipate those new wants and needs by evolving the ways in which we serve our markets.

In fact, preparing for *zeg* sits at the heart of every good strategy. In a world that is changing faster than ever before, today's strategy (which is often built on a foundation of *yesterday's* success) is obsolete even before the ink on your plan is dry. But a strategy formulated with the day after tomorrow in mind is far more likely to be sustainable over time.

Sure, you can live in the now in a business built to optimize returns this week, this month, this quarter, even this year. And you can certainly keep an eye out for tomorrow. But don't you think your strongest competitors, the industry leaders you already tend to chase from behind, the disruptors overtaking you even as you're reading this book may already have a bead on tomorrow? Or you can leapfrog both tomorrow and your competition to build a business that is ready for *zeg*.

I'm not arguing against current quarter performance. You need to survive both today and tomorrow if you want to live to see *zeg*. But too often, business leaders get so mired in the present (which given today's rate of change is practically the same as being stuck on the past) that they fail to build organizations that are ready to thrive when the not-so-distant future arrives.

Understand this—and do something about it—and

your organization just might have as many words for "the day after tomorrow" as the Inuit have for snow.

_____

July 10, 2013

STRATEGY IS CHANGE

I invite you to think about the curious annual corporate ritual known as "strategic planning," the often-rote process by which forecasts are honed, spreadsheet cells populated, templates turned into documents designed to guide a year's worth of activity.

If this sounds like a familiar grind for your organization, I'm here to tell you: *You're wasting your time.*

You don't need a strategy if you intend to spend the next 12 months (or, heaven forbid, the next 12 years) doing just a bit more of the same things you've done during the prior 12. And if this is the direction you've chosen after spending hours eyeball-deep in planning documents, then you not only *don't need* a strategy. You don't actually *have* one.

This isn't to say that you don't have a plan. You probably do, even if it's not a very good one. A plan to grow the business by 10%. A plan to show measurable, if slight, improvements in how you serve the markets you already serve, or maybe eek into a close adjacency without putting too much stress on your people or your profitability. A plan to bake a bit more efficiency into systems and structures you'd rather not change, or keep your margins from spiraling further toward zero.*

But strategy, you see, *that's* quite a different matter. Strategy is all about change.

If your strategy doesn't cause your organization and the people in it to believe something different about the business and behave differently in carrying out their business, then I'd argue you don't really have a strategy at all. Properly done, strategy moves an organization from where it is today to where it wants to be tomorrow. To a different

---

* I once worked with a client for whom "maintain margins" was the—*not a, the*—primary objective for their upcoming 12-months. No joke...

(ideally better, preferred) place it might not reach if it weren't for the hard work of a well-defined strategy.

Now, you might argue back that change isn't necessarily a condition of strategy, but a characteristic of innovation or the outcome of a well-designed change management process. If so, point me to an effective business strategy that does not have innovation as a key component. Find me that one company that boldly *refuses* to innovate; one that cares *not a bit* about exploring new ways to better serve customer needs. Sure, in practice many companies fail to do either of these things, but that failure isn't a failure of strategy so much as an inability to execute. Point me toward an organization that views change management as the end rather than the means, and I'll show you a tail wagging a dog.

Because here is an interesting corollary: *Strategy is change but not all change is strategy*. Change for the sake of change, change without focus, change without prioritization or choice is no more a strategy than a default decision to do things the same way again for yet another year in your company's lifecycle is. That is, strategy is *choice* as much as it is *change*—something that too many companies forget when creating a cover-all-the-bases-and-throw-in-the-kitchen-sink annual plan. Sure, the choice to change with focus and conviction. But also the choice to not pursue otherwise attractive opportunities that don't align with your purpose, vision and mission.

This year use your strategic planning process the way strategy is meant to be used in the first place: To change the things you do so that you can change the results you achieve.

***

November 18, 2013

A Digital Business Is A Human Business

How will becoming a more digital business help you to be a more human business?

Your answer to this question is likely to do more to shape your organization's future than any other decision you make all year because it will determine whether you remain relevant to your customers in the face of their changing expectations.

Over the past few years, many businesses have mistaken technology for transformation, when in reality technology is table stakes. It gives companies permission to play, but rarely a right to win. It's true that going digital is a vital strategic business imperative. It's obvious that everything that can be digital will be digital, that everything that can be automated will be automated. But it's the things that aren't digital, it's everything that that can't be automated (*yet!*), that will differentiate your organization from others like yours in the eyes of your customers. It's the traits that make your business (and the people in your business) uniquely human—your creativity, your empathy, your ability to resonate, your ability to relate— that will make your business worth doing business with.

Don't get me wrong. I'm not saying technology is unimportant. Far from it. I'm saying it is necessary in that it often allows an organization to strip away the routine, mundane, ineffective and inefficient elements that stifle employees' humanity and weakens relationships with customers. In fact, when you look at companies that set the bar for customer excellence—companies like Airbnb, Uber, Zappos or Lemonade—it's clear that every one of them is technology-enabled and data-driven, but ultimately human-centric. When they win, they win because they make things easier for the people who choose to do business with them (e.g., customers) and strive to make every interaction personal, meaningful, resonant and real.

This is how *you* can win too. And winning starts by getting everyone in your organization aligned around the importance of humanity in your business. Interestingly enough, you can start that process by tapping into one of the unique things we do so well as humans: *converse.*

Becoming a more human business starts with conversation—the right conversation inside your company about what this all means and how digital makes it happen, and the right conversations with your customers to reinforce the human-to-human relationships they demand of every business today.

January 7, 2019, SMART Communications 2019: The Year of the Customer, Cloud and Conversations

WE ARE THE BORG

"We are the Borg."

Star Trek fans will recognize the reference immediately as part of the standard warning issued to any alien race about to be assimilated by the collective of cybernetically-enhanced beings known as The Borg. And any routine reader of science fiction with recognize The Borg for what *they* are: a textbook example of one of science fiction's most enduring tropes, the mergers of human-and-machine known as cyborgs. And yet—although I devoured sci-fi novel after sci-fi novel throughout junior high and high school—my most memorable encounter with cyborgs (metaphorically speaking, of course) came a few years later while studying sociology at Wesleyan University in Connecticut.

As part of a course on 20th century pop culture, the professor assigned *A Cyborg Manifesto* by science and technology scholar Donna Haraway. Exactly how a dense, provocative feminist treatise qualified as pop culture, I'm not sure. But hey, it was Wesleyan, and in fairness we had more than a healthy dose of Madonna and The Terminator over the course of the semester too. Nonetheless, as its name implies, Haraway's *Manifesto* explores the notion of the cyborg broadly, as a metaphor for what humans become when their lives no longer fit so neatly within clearly defined, albeit often arbitrary, *this-or-that* boundaries. Neither man nor woman. Neither nature nor nurture. Neither physical nor virtual. Neither carbon nor silicon.

As we discussed the significance of Haraway's *Manifesto*, the professor asked the class if there were any cyborgs among us. After a few moments of blank stares, he volunteered that he himself was a cyborg, by virtue of the fact that he had an artificial heart valve. From there, students chimed in with all sorts of things—contact lenses, screws from an old fracture repair, and so on. Hardly the techno-logical marvels that would light up a hardened Trekkie's augmented eyes or set his own artificial heart valve aflut-ter, but technologies augmenting organisms, nonetheless. Bear in mind that this was back in the late 1980s.

If we were just barely cyborgs then (OK—we weren't *really,* but my professors' point was well taken—that even then it was not uncommon for the average human to be "enhanced," in one way or another, to be a *not-quite-100%* carbon-based life form), think about how far we've come *by now.* Some of us have technology implanted inside or attached to our bodies—more than ever before certainly: artificial hips and knees, prosthetic limbs, pacemakers, and Alzheimer's chips to name just a few devices.

But a much greater majority of us are augmented by technology in a somewhat different, frankly more obvious, but no less powerful way. Our mobile phones, tablets, and laptops serve as our outsourced brains, providing impor-tant reminders about where we need to be and what we need to do, opening an always-on line of communication with the people in our lives, and putting an improbably large storehouse of ideas and information (the web, our social networks) at our fingertips.

If none of this sounds quite as impressive as the cybernetic organisms that science fiction has caused us to imagine or the fabled far-futures theory of the singularity has led us to expect, I'd like to make one simple point: Even if our most common technologies are not quite inside or attached to us, *we are certainly attached to them.* Physically when we hold them in our hands or even tuck them in our pockets, but more importantly emotionally as we come to rely upon them, can't live without them, and pledge our loyalty to the Cult of Apple or Sect of Samsung.

And as anyone who keeps up with technology news already knows, we're just getting started. The market for wearables is heating up as more consumers consider health trackers, smart watches, augmented reality headsets or even interactive clothing that senses the weather and world around us. Beyond the rich-and-geeky, decidedly non-technical professions (like flight attendants, police officers, and factory floor workers) are already integrating some of these technologies into the normal course of business. And innovators continue to invent new wearable forms, dabbling with neurocams, programmable cosmetics, electronic tattoos and headsets that allow humans to interface directly with the Internet.

Still, even before most of us get comfortable with wearable computing form factors, others believe that *"insideables"* are just around the corner—*and just beneath the surface of our skin.* Smart contact lenses. Ingestible pills that carry sensors into our systems. Injectable nanorobots that go to work treating conditions and healing our bodies. Implantable interfaces like Elon Musk's Neuralink. All coming *long* before we all get subsumed by super-human artificial intelligence and become mere memory chips in a single machine-mind. (Singularity joke there, people...).

Sound like science fiction? I'm certain powerful

pocket-sized computers sounded equally improbable in the days when processors filled entire rooms.

We are the Borg, indeed. Resistance is futile.

February 12, 2014. Neuralink reference added in 2020.

THE NEW RULES NO LONGER APPLY

In times of dramatic change—times like these—it's critical that we reexamine the old rules that define how we work and jettison the ones that no longer serve their purpose. Breaking the old rules sets you on a path toward the new, the dramatic, and the different. But what you put in place to replace those old rules can be just as likely to weigh you down as they are to power you forward. Here, I'm talking about the notion of *new rules*.

An Amazon search returns more than 10,000 results among business books alone. There are new rules for work, new rules for marketing and PR, new rules for engagement, new rules for the social era, new rules for retail, green marketing, leadership, management, creating content, and selling. Damn, there are even rules for revolutionaries! I've read some of those books. Some of them are truly excellent. Packed with lots of good ideas.

And one really, really bad idea: *The idea that an old set of rules should be (sometimes even must be) replaced by some new set of rules.*

The problem with new rules is that they quickly become the old rules. What once seemed fresh, bold and maybe even disruptive becomes the new normal, "what's expected", the tired old ways "everyone does it", and sometimes even "the way we've *always* done it" (humans are indeed creatures of habit and institutions have remarkably short memories).

With new rules, we set that stage for tomorrow's tried-and-no-longer-quite-so-true standards that have long since outlived their relevance. Old ideas past their prime but carved in stone and fixed for a seeming eternity. A set of artificial constraints defined not by current market conditions, future opportunities, or next practices—but by past results, routine behaviors, and sometimes even industry-wide standards.

So how is that any different from where you started?
It isn't...

Your old rules were once new. Your new rules will soon enough be old. And they will bind you just the same.

New market conditions call for new ways of doing things, but they certainly don't call for new rules. New approaches, principles, guidelines, guideposts, frameworks, themes, theories, hypotheses, road maps, milemarkers? I wouldn't rule any of those out, and this isn't just a matter of semantics.

Guidelines are merely suggestions. Road maps offer multiple routes between points A and B, while milemarkers simply provide a means by which to measure progress. Hypotheses and theories are tested over time. Approaches, guideposts, principles, frameworks and themes are directional and extensible. None memorialize a set of rock-hard mandatories in the same way rules do.

Now, some might say rules were meant to be broken. I'm arguing rules—old rules, new rules, the very idea that your business needs to play by the rules—are *by definition* broken. Rather than replace the rules, I'd trash the rule book altogether.

But then again, you don't have to if you don't want to. There are no rules here.

_____

July 19, 2013

99 Problems But Resources Ain't One

et's say you're faced with a choice between the thing you've always done and some new thing you might consider doing. It could be anything, so long as it represents change—shifting more of your marketing spend into digital, ramping up your ecommerce presence, adding a new retail location, launching a new product or service, expanding into an adjacent territory or market, piloting a new business model, spinning off a new company. If you weigh the options, sigh, and lament that you quite simply don't have the *"resources"* to get it done, you're using one of the most common excuses in business. And like just about every other executive who has used it, you're placing blame where it doesn't belong.

When you say that you don't have the resources to accomplish something—the money, the people, the time—what you're really saying is that you aren't willing to make that thing a *priority*.

You see, in just about every area of business, we've moved beyond the state of *haves vs have nots* and into a state of *wills vs will nots*. Where there's a will, as they say, there *is* a way. The challenge is that for many executives, there's not a *will*—there's a *won't*. And that *won't* stands *in the way* of real progress.

Resources are rarely the issue. *Priorities are.*

I appreciate that there are, indeed, some practical real-world constraints. But for any business above a certain size, *the money is there*; you're just choosing to invest it in other things. *The people are there*; you've just chosen to allocate them to other tasks, or you've simply chosen not to invest in helping them develop the skills they'd need to take on new responsibilities. *The time is there*; you're just using it for other things. Lack of money, lack of people, lack of time all boil down to just one thing: Lack of priorities. And, left too long, a lack of priorities results in a lack of growth.

What is it about business that drives us to forgo prioritization for mere allocation? Is it fear? Complacency? Outmoded beliefs?

At the end of the day, it's not the things you *have* that define your business or career. It's the things you *do*. It's not really the lack of resources that hold us back. It's the poor choices we make about how to invest those resources. If you want to move your business forward, to seize the opportunity to do new things, to say you *will* and find a way to make it happen, then you need to start with one simple step: *Get your priorities straight.*

November 6, 2013

INNOVATION MYTHBUSTING

I f there's a poster child for innovation, it's Thomas Edison. And if there's a slogan scrawled across his poster, it's probably his often-cited quote, "I have not failed. I've just found 10,000 ways that won't work," which is generally believed to relate to his work on the light bulb.

If you're looking for a nicely packaged call for the power of perseverance, the rewards received for taking risks, or the benefits of having a go-get-'em can-do attitude you really can't do much better than these words of wisdom from the man who gave the world the light bulb, the telegraph, the phonograph and motion pictures. It's little wonder that innovation pundits love to trot out this oldie but goodie to inspire business leaders to lean further into the future, take chances, accommodate failure, and adopt an innovation mindset.

Granted, Edison may never have actually said these words (although generally attributed to the inventor, they've never been confirmed as his own). For that matter— despite what many believe—he didn't really *invent* the light bulb, arguably the object most often associated with his name and the icon that has become the de facto visual shorthand for "great idea", but an invention that predates his work to *improve upon it* by roughly 50 years. So not to take anything away from the man (his accomplishments are many), but the *10,000 ways that won't work* story is a *myth*. An innovation creation myth of sorts, from which the permission to innovate springs forth.

But neither a questionable quote nor a faulty fact points to the real issue here. You see, as inspirational as it may seem, the *10,000 ways* quote doesn't actually provide a formula for successful innovation (sorry experts!). By any measure, no matter what the end result, 10,000 tries for every successful completion make for a very poor track record. 10,000 to 1 is a ratio that favors quantity over quality and suggests that the answer lies in generating *more* ideas when in reality it lies in generating *good* ideas. *More* and *good* are not mutually exclusive of course, but imagine the resources a 10,000-idea torrent would consume in your own business. And imagine how long it could take to generate, filter, and then find the (arguably) few ideas even worth testing. Even with an open innovation model in which the ideas may come fast and furious, the follow up effort of giving each idea the appropriate level of consideration is hardly a trivial task.

Maybe businesses had the luxury of time back around the turn of the last century, but a dozen years into *this* century the frenzied pace of change means that time is of the essence. Innovators need fast. Innovators need efficient. Innovators need to find the one thing that works without having to wade through the 10,000 that won't.

So, 10,000 ways is a myth that might encourage an otherwise risk averse leader to consider innovation, but it's not one that serves today's companies particularly well.

That said, this type of myth may actually be the lesser of two evils.

At a bare minimum, the *10,000 ways* quote speaks to the importance of trying again and again, until you ultimately break through the roadblock that sits between you and your goal. It's benign compared to the many innovation myths that have the exact opposite effect: The effect of holding businesses back.

I'm talking about the misconceptions about what innovation is, where it sits in an organization, how it gets done, and what it's meant to accomplish. Now, I'm no expert on innovation, but I know the damage that believing in these myths can do when it comes to a corporation's innovation efforts, so I'd like to run down some of *these* myths and bust them one by one.

Myth #1: Innovation Is Just Ideas.

Edisonian math aside, ideas are indeed important to innovation. What's less clear is whether your innovation effort will require three, 300 or 30,000 ideas in order to get to a single solution. They key word there is *solution*. Innovation isn't about generating ideas. It's about finding solutions. To create value, innovation must focus on solving a clearly defined challenge (for the company or, even better, for its customers) through applied creativity, a clear path to implementation, and an eye on accountability. If your company's attempts at innovation amount to little more than shiny object-chasing and trivial distractions from the matter at hand, it's not because your ideas aren't any good (they may be, they may not be). It's because you haven't kept your purpose in mind.

Myth #2: Innovation Is an Event.

When companies confuse ideas with innovation, they tend to rely too heavily on event-based innovation exercises like brainstorming sessions, hackathons or executive off-sites. Sure, they can be fun, the participants leave jazzed, and the organizers feel like they've amassed a handful of new ideas. But within a day or two, everyone goes back to business as usual. Plenty ventured, nothing gained. Why? Because real results require an always-on approach, sustainable processes, and platforms that empower your people (and in the social era, your customers and partners) to function as a well-tuned innovation capability.

Myth #3: R&D Owns Innovation.

R&D absolutely plays a key role in product innovation, but even on that front it can be a mistake for the customer-facing functions in an organization (like marketing, sales, and customer support, at the very least) to relinquish their own roles in making sure innovation is market-focused. But that's not the only reason to debunk the notion of R&D-only innovation. Done right, innovation creates competitive advantage by differentiating your business across *all* core areas—from strategy, sales and customer service, to people, product, and process (not to mention everything in between). I can't think of many R&D organizations that would prioritize improving marketing efficacy by employing new digital strategies, increasing company cash flow by adopting an untried approach to collections, or increasing knowledge-sharing and productivity by fostering a more collaborative mindset across the organization. In fact, I can think of exactly zero R&D departments where this would be the case.

So, who really owns innovation? Everybody in the organization—at least as it pertains to delivering excellence in their own areas of subject matter expertise. But even better, beyond their own areas of subject matter expertise. Who's to say an accounting clerk might not have a creative solution to a supply chain problem or branding challenge?

Myth #4: Innovation Is All iPhones.

This is my shorthand for a common innovation objection—one that is closely related to the R&D myth and hinges upon the notions that all innovation is radical or disruptive, and that all innovation aims to bring bold new products into the world.

A few years back, I was doing some work with the innovation lead at a large consumer packaged goods company. In his role, he considered it his job to bring to life not only innovations that were new to the world or even new to his category, but also those that were simply new to his company. Good thinking. No matter what business you're in, success requires you to manage a diverse portfolio of radical, substantial and incremental innovations that together strike the right balance between risks and rewards. In fact, it can often be the incremental, bread-and-butter changes that add up to lasting value. Remember: Edison didn't invent the light bulb; he improved on it. Yet a century later, his is the name we most closely associate with our bright present.

Taking things one step further (myth #4.5 perhaps), it might even be a mistake to think of new products as core to innovation (whether radical, substantial, or incremental) at all. Today, businesses are more likely to have greater impact by focusing their efforts on creating new value through experiences (products + services + participation) or new business models, even where the product itself is essentially unchanged. For example, Zipcar didn't change the car but they did introduce a new model by which urban dwellers can access one when the need it; Netflix didn't reinvent the DVD but they did change the model by which movie fans rent them (before innovating away from requiring their customers to rent them at all).

Business model is the new iPhone—and your company or industry may not be aching for its next iPhone-caliber *product* innovation, but its basic business model might benefit from some shaking up (from the inside out).

Myth #5: Innovation Is Out of Reach.

This one comes in a variety of forms, but the two objections I hear most often boil down to *my industry isn't interesting enough* and *but I'm not a visionary*. Neither holds water, in my opinion. One of Clayton Christensen's most popular examples of disruption pits upstart, low-end rebar manufacturers against established, high-end sheet metal fabricators. I'm sure the steel industry is fascinating to some, but it's hardly the stuff of next generation entrepreneurial day dreams. No business is so boring as to be insusceptible to change.

Then we have the popular mythology that surrounds a modern-day Edison like the late Steve Jobs. Jobs was a man who foresaw the future not just once but several times over, remaking industries as diverse as home computing, entertainment and telecommunications. How can anyone compare, particularly if she's a merely mortal accountant, attorney, corporate program manager, or marketing strategist?

Here's how: Innovation doesn't require you to understand the future, so much as it requires you to understand your customers' needs. I know Jobs was famous for disregarding customer needs in favor of creating new-to-the-world products that would ultimately create unrealized customer demand. Fantastic, but for most of us, defining more effective or more efficient ways to meeting *known or clearly emerging* customer demands—whether your customers are external to your business or internal to it, as they may be for those who work in finance, corporate communications, project management or other ostensibly meat-and-potatoes functions—lies at the heart of sustained, always-on innovation. In short, if you can conceive of a better way to do even just one small aspect of your job and have just enough drive to do something about it, you are playing a role in business innovation. It may not be iTunes, iPhone or iPad-sexy, but it is just as vital to the ongoing success of your company.

Myth #6: Innovation Is Optional.

In today's business environment, it's difficult enough to sustain momentum, all-consuming just to maintain the status quo. Can we really afford to invent the future when there's so much to get done just to keep pace with the present? The truth is, you can't afford *not* to.

For businesses—and businesspeople—who believe

that innovation is a nice to have more than a must have, a flavor of the month more than a nourishing staple of their diet, this myth is the most damaging of all. It's the one that gives permission to get by with an occasional and ineffective check-the-box-for-innovation brainstorm, to abdicate responsibility to the guys in the goggles, to place the promise of innovation just out of reach. It's the one that causes companies to fall behind, fall out of favor, and fall apart in the face of disruption.

Disruption is only disruption when it comes from outside your organization and lies beyond your control. Otherwise, it's transformation. And innovation is the engine for transformation. It is essential. Just as Peter Drucker (or Milan Kundera, or maybe both—yet another disputed quote) contends that innovation is one of only two basic functions of a business, former Proctor & Gamble chairman A.G. Lafley has said, "Innovation is the central job of every leader—business unit managers, functional leaders, and the CEO."

Now that's a mandate worth repeating 10,000 or so times over.

*   *   *

Now, while I don't suppose there are 9,994 additional harmful myths that throw businesses off track when it comes to innovation, I do expect there are more than the simple six I've laid out here. This is where you come in. What other myths, misconceptions or roadblocks are holding your company back when it comes to turning innovation into a competitive advantage? And what can you do to bust them?

———————————

October 29, 2012

50 QUESTIONS TO SPARK STRATEGIC INNOVATION

I believe that strategy is change and I know that change can be hard. But *getting started* shouldn't be. You just need to be willing to ask the right kinds of questions, the answers to which will prompt you to reimagine every area of your business from your value proposition to your product set, from your ideal customer to your unseen competitor, from your strengths to your stumbling blocks, from what to keep to what to kill. So, with this in mind, I took just ten minutes to make a list of 50 (*50!*) questions that have the potential to spark strategic thinking and innovation. Here's what I came up with.

1. Who are we?

2. Who do we *want* to be?

3. Who do we serve?

4. Who do our customers think we are?

5. Who do we *want* our customers to think we are?

6. What business(es) are we in?

7. What business(es) *should* we be in?

8. What businesses(es) *must* we be in within the next five years?

9. What business(es) should we *not* be in?

10. What do we believe?

11. What truly makes us different?

12. What cannot be imitated?

13. Where is the one place our competition would never go?

14. What would we like to be remembered for?

15. Where are we strongest?

16. Where are we weakest?

17. What existing capabilities or assets can be applied in new ways?

18. What new capabilities or assets are required?

19. Why do customers choose us?

20. Why do customers choose to *leave* us?

21. What customer needs do we *actually* meet?

22. What would customers value *more*?

23. What other options (especially beyond the obvious) meet similar customer needs?

24. What other markets have similar needs that we could serve (but aren't serving today)?

25. What else do customers do before, during, and after they buy our product?

26. What customer need remains unmet?

27. What job can customers *not* get done today?

28. How could we super-serve the customers nobody else wants?

29. What could we do that would defy expectations?

30. What beliefs about our business no longer serve us well—what should replace them?

31. Of the things we do today, which are (or will soon be) obsolete?

32. Where is the white space?

33. How else could we create value?

34. How can we make or do this better?

35. How has someone outside our industry solved the same problem?

36. What do other companies outside our industry or beyond our markets offer?

37. Who could we partner with to enter new markets?

38. Who could we partner with to provide new solutions in existing markets?

39. If we could start again, what would we be?

40. What trends are most likely to shape our future?

41. What's likely to disrupt us?

42. What would it look like if we were to become the disruptor?

43. How is technology changing our industry?

44. How can *we* use technology to change our industry?

45. How will new competitors be different or better?

46. How would [Elon Musk, Jeff Bezos, Larry Page, etc.] approach our market?

47. How can we make the process of buying and using our product simpler?

48. What new distribution channels or ways to purchase should we explore?

49. What constraints exist, and how can we reduce or remove them?

50. How can we reimagine a product as a service (or a service as a product)?

Naturally, you won't need (*or want*) to sit your team down and run them through all 50—and if you take ten minutes of your own time, I'd bet you could come up with 50 more. But really, all you need is one, the answer to which causes you to ask just one more question. Perhaps the question that matters most: *"What's possible?"*

_____

April 22, 2015

Soothsayers & Naysayers

The world is divided between soothsayers and naysayers. Visionaries and reactionaries. Agents of change and keepers of the peace. Clairvoyants gazing into crystal balls and collectors lovingly rearranging mementos in curio cabinets.

While it takes all types to make the world go around, I know which I'd rather have in charge of my organization's business transformation, innovation initiatives, or even the entire strategic planning process. *Which would you?*

The distinction between the two—and for me, the advantage of one over the other—comes down to a simple matter of perspective. But this simple shift in perspective truly makes a world of difference.

Naysayers See Problems from the Standpoint of the Present

At best, their focus is on improving upon the current state. These are the people who build their plans around safe, incremental growth (*10% growth never got anyone fired, right?*); that eschew the truly new for a bit more of the same. At worst, they simply aim to maintain the status quo. These are the folks who ignore new competitors, balk at disruptors, deny that the assumptions upon which their businesses are built have become the quicksand that threatens to suck their businesses under.

When faced with radical innovations or unconventional ideas, all they see are obstacles. They're very good at explaining why breakthrough ideas won't work, *can't work*. They don't just believe this. They *know* it. And they're more than happy to *prove* it to you.

Soothsayers Solve Problems from the Perspective of the Future

Rather than starting with an understanding of the current state, they begin with a vision for a preferred future state. They go beyond what they know to be true to consider what they imagine to be possible. When facing radical innovations and unconventional ideas, they don't see obstacles. *They see opportunities.*

Soothsayers do more than just maintain the business they have. They create the business they want. They're very good at determining how breakthrough ideas could work, *should* work, *will* work. And they're more than happy to *show* you.

Now, some might say that any good business needs a healthy blend of both: hard-nosed realists to balance out the starry-eyed visionaries. Maybe that's true. *Who am I to say no?* But when the naysayers outweigh and outvote the soothsayers in any organization, the result

71

isn't safety. It's *stasis*. And that's the riskiest position of all.

September 17, 2013

Stories Drive Transformation Success

When Sree Sreenivasan was Chief Digital Officer at New York's Metropolitan Museum of Art, he told a writer for the Huffington Post that the future of all business is about storytelling. It's telling (pun intended) that the man charged with bringing his venerable institution into the technology-driven 21st century would point to a something as old fashioned as storytelling when envisioning the future of business. Telling, yes, but hardly surprising.

If storytelling isn't new (it's not), it has certainly come centerstage in this age of content marketing, the humanization of business, and the drive for differentiation as technology strips away both barriers to entry and points of analog interaction. Stories have always played an important role in changing beliefs and behaviors, and now as just about every organization embarks on a transformation journey (digital or otherwise), it's more important than ever that leaders employ the right tools to change the beliefs and behaviors of the key stakeholders—customers, partners, employees, shareholders, boards, etc.—throughout their business ecosystem. Storytelling fits the bill.

Transformation is vital to those organizations that want to win in the world of business today. Stories are vital to those who want to win at transformation. Indeed, *"Those who tell the stories rule the world." (a* Hopi proverb or Plato quotable, depending on which sources you choose to believe).

Here are just five ways in which stories can play a strategic role in business transformation:

Stories Stick

They answer: *What Must I Know?*

This is hardly new news for anyone who remembers the now-classic business book *Made To Stick* or knows that Carnegie Mellon research once proved that stories are not only more memorable than data, but that stories *alone* are more memorable than stories *plus data*. Clearly, when a business message is so important that you want recipients (either inside or outside your organization) to remember it and repeat it, it makes sense to put stories to work. And as far as important messages go, the message that you are taking your company on a transformation journey ranks among the most important messages you're likely to deliver as a leader.

Stories Add Emotional Weight

They answer: *Why Should I Care?*

While facts can *sometimes* speak for themselves, even the most hardened business person has an intuitive, emotional side that must be engaged by leaders looking to inspire (key word there) new beliefs and behaviors. Stories that engage the emotions instead of the intellect do a better job of creating buy-in among the very people that carry the weight of responsibility for delivering change at all levels of the business. Or, as author <u>Simon Sinek</u> might say, stories give people their *why*.

Stories Help Us Make Sense

They answer: *What's In It For Me?*

Exponential change and our companies' efforts to transform to meet new marketplace demands create significant gaps between knowledge and understanding. Artificial intelligence and robotics will automate a significant number of jobs—*but what does that mean for me?* We are shifting toward a gig economy in which the nature of work is more dynamic than ever before—*how will that effect my career?* My company is making a shift from product to service, from pipeline to platform, from analog to digital—*why is this important and what will it look like?* Stories are a powerful way to provide the context people need in order for them to understand not only the methods of change but also the meaning.

Stories Show the Way

They answer: *Where Are We Going? How Will We Get There?*

Stories—with their basic beginning-middle-end structure—are a highly effective way to bring a transformation journey to life, dramatize the ideal end-state, and highlight all the steps along the way. This is why futurists often use stories to make theoretical scenarios feel plausible, practical, and concrete. Transformation stories ground your stakeholders in the current state, help them envision the future state, and *'take them with you'* as you navigate the road from one to the other. And they do this in a way that feels more real and more relevant than any data-driven business presentation can.

Stories Are Shared

They answer: *What Part Can I Play?*

People certainly love to tell stories to others. Memorable stories make the rounds. These things are true, but I'm actually talking about something else too. Done right, strategic stories *involve* listeners as participants in the plot, are truly *shared* in the sense that everyone plays a part in advancing the action and feels ownership over the outcomes. By laying out an open and inclusive business narrative, leaders provide others in the organization with an effective model for telling *their own* stories in support of that narrative.

Tell me, what's *your* transformation story? Better yet, don't tell *me*. Tell your team and take them on the journey with you.

April 25, 2016

WHAT YOU'LL LEARN WHEN YOU LEARN TO CODE

Despite decades spent in and around digital—including seven or so working inside technology startups—I never learned to code. Sure, there was that one three-day-course my parents enrolled me in during the summer between fifth and sixth grades, but this was way back in the 70s (long before my career began) and the process of programming a simple trivia game by typing arcane language into a machine that didn't even have a monitor (you had to *print* the code on *paper* to debug it) hardly inspired me to pursue a coding career. And sure, I know enough basic HTML to tweak a setting here or there on my own website. But I wouldn't say I've learned to code.

Until yesterday. And frankly, it was a long-time coming.

I'm not sure what took me so long. Whenever I've wanted to truly understand the effects of a given technology on business, I've simply *done* it. It's why I signed up for my first online service. Worked at streaming media startups. Launched my blog. Rushed to try MySpace, Facebook, Second Life (don't judge), Twitter, Instagram, Vine (RIP) and countless platforms that have long since come and gone. And when clients want to understand how their employees or customers use new technologies, I'm always inclined to teach them how to use those technologies for themselves, whether that means sitting beside a senior executive as he types his first tweet or turning hundreds of members of a global leadership team into "consumer" content creators over the course of a week.

But coding? I've left it to the coders.

So finally, yesterday, I spent a day with a small group of mid-career professionals (mostly ad agency types), going through a learn-to-code-in-a-day program—a 10-hour curriculum that promised attendees with no technical skills that they would be coding a proper mobile app within a single day.

Precisely as promised, after a whirlwind tour through the fundamentals of HTML, CSS and JavaScript; some poking around through public libraries of open source code; line-level (literally line-level) thinking about how geolocation works; and a lesson in how simple it is to make a design responsive to work across multiple devices, I was the proud maker of a basic app that let users check in at a given location but only after validating that the user was, in fact, at that actual location.* My little app—a minimally viable product if ever there was one—would hardly keep anyone in Silicon Valley awake at night but all-in-all I'd say it's not half-bad for a day's worth of work.

Did I learn to code? Well, sort of. It would be more accurate to say that I learned *about* code. How it works,

---

* Imagine a rudimentary Foursquare rip-off.

what it does, why it matters and the part it plays in digital business strategy. I learned what it's like to actually *do* something digital at its most basic level.

I'd also say that when it comes to code, this is exactly what every digital business leader needs to know.

While it's not inconceivable that some folks who go through a program like Code in a Day get bitten by the bug, and go on to complete multi-month courses that will power them through to a new career in software development, the more likely outcome is that these already accomplished professionals—these strategists, account directors, entrepreneurs and accountants—will simply go back to their work-a-day realities, doing what they've trained a lifetime to do.

But as they do, they'll do so with a better understanding of the technologies that underlie the applications they rely on to deliver solutions, a newfound respect for the work the technical team toils away at late into the night, and a far greater appreciation for what it takes—at the absolute, most fundamental level—to translate even the biggest-picture digital vision into a fully-formed reality.

These things rarely come from reading trade publications, pontificating at the podium, or running even the world's most sophisticated models. They come from hands-on experience. And it is exactly this kind of hands-on experience that has the power to spark the cultural shifts that transform organizations and the individuals who lead them, as it teaches not simply a new skillset but also the importance of adopting a new mindset. You'll gain a new vocabulary by which to describe your business, you'll gain new tools for collaboration between the rapidly converging business and technical sides of your organization, and you'll gain keener insights into digital strategy and execution.

In other words, *doing* digital bridges the gap between merely *talking* digital and actually *being* digital. And in a world where *being* digital separates the winners from the losers, *doing* digital can make the difference between

NEW NORMAL

leading your organization's transformation and getting left behind as your organization transforms without you.

And this is what you'll really learn when you learn to code.

_____

August 24, 2014

THE
DISCOVERY
OF
WATER

Marshall McLuhan once pointed out that *"Fish did not discover water,"* going on to explain that, *"In fact, because they are completely immersed in it, they live unaware of its existence. Similarly, when a conduct is normalized by a dominant cultural environment, it becomes invisible."*

We are all immersed so deeply in something that it becomes invisible to us. To those of us who swim in digital transformation, what's new is what's normal.

We already live and work in a world where the largest media companies create no content, the most valuable taxi service has no fleet, and one of the biggest brands in hospitality doesn't own a single room let alone an entire hotel full of rooms.*

Well, of course! And why shouldn't this be the case?

I spend so much time thinking about the digital future that I have little difficulty imagining a world where artificial intelligence, virtual reality, and connected *everything* are all part of the environment.

Do you mean we're not already living in this world today?

What's more, I feel this way despite the fact that I am, technically speaking, a digital immigrant—albeit one who, like the so-called boiling frog, was immersed in the water early enough that I barely noticed as my cool pool became a bubbling sea of change. Yet, I work hard to remain aware that what might be the normal

---

* You've likely seen these points made before, credited to marketing strategist Tom Goodwin and his March 2015 article in TechCrunch. I published the original version of this essay on my blog one month earlier. I'm not sure who influenced who. I'd like to believe that great minds think alike—and to be fair, Tom said it better and I'm willing to accept that he said it first, somewhere, because he's a supersmart dude.

environment to me can appear to be an alien landscape to others.

This is important, because inside the fishbowl, it's easy to lose a sense of perspective. And when advising others on how to navigate change or deal with disruption, it's actually an *outside* perspective that matters most.

This is a theme I've returned to a number of times over the years—reminding early adopters to remember that they are indeed ahead of the curve before flitting off to some next new thing, urging experts to become (or at least think like) beginners, and making a case for considering matters through the eyes of someone who takes the opposite point of view.

And it is, of course, the point McLuhan is making when he points out that fish did not (could not possibly) discover water, because discovery of one thing requires knowledge of another.

Personally, I try to keep this in mind when guiding clients through transformation. It might be difficult to see how analog executives struggle to embrace transformation because to me the signs of change are all around us and clear to see. It's often just as difficult for these executives (for people in general) to see the opportunities that lie beyond their boundaries. This is why, for every time I urge a client to *"come on in, the water's fine,"* I also make a point of sprouting legs and strolling from the sea in order to discover some common ground

_____

February 12, 2015

BECOME A BEGINNER

Yesterday afternoon, I sat down to talk shop with a fellow consultant—let's call him Chris.* As the business conversation wound down and talk turned to trivial bits of this and that, Chris mentioned that he has recently begun learning how to play the guitar. What he said next gave me one of those insights that sits at the intersection of *aha* and *but of course*. Chris told me how valuable it has been for him to be a beginner at something. So much so that next he may teach himself how to write code.

We're *all* expert at something. Some of you reading this may be strategy experts, marketing experts, innovation experts or digital transformation experts. Others may

---

* Because that's his actual name.

have deep expertise in technology, engineering, analytics, manufacturing, accounting, law, medicine, or just about any other profession or business competency.

Expertise is good. Expertise is necessary.

When I choose a lawyer, doctor, or accountant, I *expect* them to be at the top of their game; I'd imagine you do too. When I bring a business analyst or data scientist into a client engagement, I expect that they have a firm grasp of current best practices and can deliver the value my clients expect.

But being a beginner is necessary too.

Why?

Because with expertise comes the curse of knowledge—the inability to see the subject of our expertise from the perspective of less expert others; a jaded perspective that suffers from a deeply ingrained set of assumptions about how things are and how they are meant to be; a distorted view through an overused lens; a less-than-helpful lack of empathy for the novice.

I often note this kind of thing among my peers in

technology and transformation—the hyper-connected insiders always on the hunt for the next big thing, who often declare a tool, technology or platform old news long before the mainstream population has adopted it as their own. I've been guilty of this myself. And as someone with a 30-year track record, I can sometimes forget that the concepts, approaches, and processes that seem obvious to me might be totally alien to an executive who hasn't spent a career thinking about the nuances of business transformation.

Becoming a beginner reminds you what it's like to view something through a new lens. What it's like to tackle a fresh challenge. How it feels to accomplish something for the first time. And frankly, how it feels to struggle with a concept, task, or skill that you haven't yet mastered. Becoming a beginner reminds you that expertise is a gift—and also a curse. A thing hard won over time and through a daunting amount of hard work. And a thing to keep in check by constantly reexamining it as if it were something truly new. Because to others, *it is.*

So, *what* should you begin? Almost anything will do—pick up an instrument you've never played or a paint brush you've never held. Learn more about wine, film-making or even bookkeeping. Whatever suits your style.

For certain, any of these things will open your eyes to new possibilities. Or reinforce the fact that the world has never been so ripe with change. That just about every day brings new developments, disruptive changes, revolutionary or even just evolutionary ideas that bear consideration. Go through your work day with your blinders off and become a beginner at all the things that lie just outside your core area of expertise.

You just might become a better expert in the process.

August 21, 2012

ABOUT GREG

GREG VERDINO is a highly regarded authority on *"the digital now."* He is known for his uncanny ability to forecast trends, spot the difference between fads and the future, and empower organizations to thrive in the face of exponential change.

Greg's perspectives have been shaped by 30 years spent working at the forefront of change, during which time he has advised hundreds of organizations including more than 50 of the Fortune 500; has served in senior leadership positions at a half-dozen technology start-ups; and has launched innovative products, lines of business, and divisions from within traditional companies. Through his work speaking, writing, and consulting on business transformation and always-on adaptability, he helps business leaders build thriving, future-ready companies.

Greg is the author of *microMARKETING: Get Big Results by Thinking and Acting Small* (McGraw-Hill, 2010) and *Never Normal* (you're reading it, right now). As the co-creator of *The Adapt Manifesto*, Greg is leading a movement to align leaders around a core set of principles that help organizations reliably and repeatedly adapt to the changing environment in which they operate. Throughout his career, he has served as a go-to expert for a wide range of media outlets including Bloomberg Business, CNN, eMarketer, the New York Times, Raconteur and the Wall Street Journal. He is a professional member of the National Speakers Association who has spoken at hundreds of corporate and association events throughout North America, in Latin America, Europe, Asia and Africa—and online.

He lives on Long Island with his family and the world's most disobedient cat.

EVEN MORE GREG

Also by Greg

microMARKETING:

Get Big Results by Thinking and Acting Small

Get in Touch

www.gregverdino.com

me@gregverdino.com

twitter.com/gregverdino

linkedin.com/in/gregverdino

Or sign up for my newsletter at

getrevue.co/profile/gregverdino

The Adapt Manifesto

If you enjoyed this book, you'll probably be interested in the Adapt Manifesto—a movement to align leaders around seven values and ten practices that help organizations repeatedly and reliably adapt to and thrive in the face of unrelenting change. *Adapt* is more philosophy about change than strategy for change; a set of guidelines for how change happens rather than a prescription for what that change should be. Learn more and join the movement at **www.adaptmanifesto.org**.